C3:

CHRIST CENTERED COACHING

C3:
CHRIST CENTERED COACHING

≫ *Utilizing Faith to Impact Athletes* ≪

BY
DR. D. B. HOLSTEIN

Table of Contents

≫ 1 ≪

THE BEGINNINGS

The echo of the bouncing basketballs had long ago dissipated into the musty gymnasium air. Practice had completed almost two hours earlier on this frigid February evening at the small Midwestern community college. The players had long since left the facility for their evening activities.

As the young second-year head coach sat in the stands watching the janitor pace up and down with his dust mop cleaning the hardwood floor, his thoughts were flooded with questions concerning the remainder of the season. He had been an assistant coach for sixteen years in this nationally recognized junior college program, sitting one seat to the right. Being the major decisionmaker and leader, though, was a totally different experience. He had often thought during the first year-and-a-half that one could view and evaluate the decisions of any head coach, but until one has walked in those shoes, he could never understand the responsibility and accountability faced each day.

One day earlier, the coach had made the decision that the relationship with one of his better players must be dissolved. Therefore, after much discussion with his staff, this player was eliminated from the team for the remainder of the season. To complicate the situation, the team was not doing very well from a competitive standpoint, morale was low, and it appeared there would be very little chance of winning another regional championship, which would signify the team as one of the top twenty-four junior college basketball programs in the country. This accomplishment had happened seven of the previous eight years.

The coach remembered his playing days, and the bonding and camaraderie that occurred on a team striving for a goal. Back then the coach was viewed as the authority, not only because of the position he held but also because of the knowledge and teaching expertise experience had given him. The players' perceptions were those of respect and trust. The times had changed, and as the years flowed by it appeared that perceptions of effective coaching behaviors had changed from a player viewpoint. There seemed to be more questioning, and players were more concerned about individual accomplishments than working together and achieving a collective goal. The coach had become more of a manager of personalities, rather than simply someone who automatically knew what was best for the team. The approach of what was best for the entire group did not seem to fit in a day when instant gratification and individual needs were of utmost importance.

The next six weeks would be a difficult process. Would the perception of the coach change in the players' view and, if so, would that affect their individual performance and satisfaction within the team dynamic? A deeper issue would be this: What would the players' perceptions of the coach as their leader be, after this decision? Would the players view this decision as one that would better the team? More importantly, could this issue have been avoided with a balanced vision, by creating a culture of effective communication and of valuing the individual for the good of the group?

Six weeks later, his team did capture another regional championship. It all worked out for the benefit of the team;

however, these questions were still very prevalent in the coach's mind as he accepted the championship trophy on that mid-March night. If you haven't guessed already, that young coach was me.

* * * * *

In my youth, I can remember sitting in the front row of my father's church. It was there that I not only learned the doctrines of Christianity, but establishment principles such as authority orientation, timeliness, wisdom of the elder, elements of discipline, the art of paying attention, and humility, among others.

Additionally, during that period of my life, I was introduced to and developed an extreme love of sports, particularly football, basketball, and baseball. I can remember playing sports with my brother at the age of five. I liked all the "major sports" at that time, but as the years went on and through the experience of a childhood accident which blinded me in my right eye, I began to gravitate to basketball. And as I grew up in the basketball-crazy state of Indiana, the lure became overwhelming.

Those two defining foundational blocks—church, and my love of sports—have had the deepest impact in providing a base for what I perceive as right and good. The repetitive consistency of these two areas of my life shaped the course of my youth, teen, and adult years.

The impact of listening to the gospel every Sunday and Wednesday for the first thirteen years of my life provided me a spiritual foundation that has never left. However, I did not always understand the application of the spiritual life into my daily activities until later. Although through the years I have strayed, and not necessarily applied the foundation in the Word that my mother and father laid for me on a day-to-day basis, I have always known that it is this foundation that has carried me through in my relational and professional experiences in good times and in adversity. In addition, the life lessons that playing and coaching sports taught me were a valuable tool, as I began to align my thinking about the common challenges faced daily in the spiritual and athletic world.

I can honestly say that I am an everyday man who has been fortunate enough to experience success along with failure in my playing days in junior high, high school, junior college, and four-year college basketball. My professional career has been exclusively focused on administrating athletic departments and coaching at the two-year college level. I believe I have learned, through these successes and failures, valuable lessons that have shaped my life and assisted me in becoming a better human being and a witness for the Lord.

I am not famous, and never have aspired to be. I have been immersed in two-year college athletics for almost four decades. I have learned to understand that this is the environment the Lord wanted me in, to witness through my understanding and maturity in the Word of God which has been ever-evolving for the past twelve years. My experiences have led me to believe that the competitive nature of the athletic arena seems at times to conflict with the teachings of Jesus. The often-volatile nature of the athletic arena and the teachings of Jesus Christ when he was upon the earth do not seem to be in alignment, from our human perspective. Compassion, empathy, selflessness, and humility just don't seem evident in what we see with many of our coaches, athletes, and parents in today's world. What we often perceive are individuals who display characteristics such as arrogance, selfishness, self-serving, and team-demeaning individuality without any awareness of the damage that they are creating around them. Because of this we ask: Can we be competitive, yet display a personality different from what we are witnessing today in our world of athletics?

How do we, as coaches, survive and even flourish in an environment that often seems so chaotic and out of balance?

Those questions are the motivating inspiration for this manuscript. In the following chapters I hope to provide insight, as someone who has spent his entire professional career in coaching and athletics. These experiences, observations, and insights, I'm sure, are somewhat typical of all levels of coaching. There are many of us coaches out there at all levels who need a defining moment in our lives to balance the seemingly increasing chaos in our athletic community. This chaos—in the form of inappropriate, violent, and unethical behavior—not only pervades our athletes but is being seen in coaches, parents, and other stakeholders within the field of sport.

My hope is that these violent and unethical actions are not becoming the norm, and that through this witness some sense and definition for you, the coach, will crystallize—and that you will be able to transfer that behavior to the young men and women you teach.

This book has been a labor of love, based on my professional and personal observations and experiences in the athletic arena. My prayer is that you will find it not only informing and sensible, but also that you will be able to apply it in your day-to-day interaction with your athletes.

≫ 2 ≪

THE CENTER OF ALL THINGS

*Commit to the L*ORD *whatever you do,*
and your plans will succeed

— Proverbs 16:3

The Foundation

Certainly, when one thinks about what core values drive their leadership model, many traits jump out that should be included. Before I expound on these values, I would like to point out that, even though it is not defined as a value, I sincerely believe that often the better-adjusted leaders have a spiritually centered mentality that helps create balance. It is important to note that when we as individuals look at values that are good to have, it can be said that all of them are found in the person of Jesus Christ. The journey to become more Christlike in our daily lives, both from a personal and professional sense, is a lifelong quest that takes daily self-evaluation on how one treats others, and a consistent diet of correct interpretation of Scripture and how it can be applicable to our daily living. This Scripture analysis allows a leader to develop a relaxed state and a humanness about themselves, in their day-to-day dealings with the ones they love and in their professional relationships.

Along the journey of my coaching career, I was fortunate enough to be inducted into the National Junior College Athletic Association Region 4 (Illinois) Hall of Fame as a coach/athletic director. Although I am not one who receives momentum from praise and approbation, it was satisfying in the fact that this leadership style—not only in dealing with young people through my coaching endeavors but also with my colleagues—was viewed as effective, and this validated my journey.

My acceptance speech was entitled "Anatomy of an Award." The very first core value that I believe is critical to be well adjusted in any leader is humility. Therefore, I spoke of my professional mentor, assistant coaches, players, and volunteers of the program, collaborative departments I worked with, upper level administration, the president that hired me and the programs booster club at length. My intent was to try and help everyone understand that although I was the recipient of the reward, the journey had to do with many well-meaning and loyal people. It was a collaboration of many who had my best interests at heart, in order for this to be accomplished. To take this a step further, I believe and try to live by the truth of the Word, that any success that I have had is a gift from God. He placed the right resources in both people and situations for me to be in an environment for success. It is by his grace and his grace only that I have been allowed to pursue a career that I have enjoyed.

Secondly, I believe one must have a true passion for what they do. Without passion, there is no intrinsic drive to achieve. All motivation then comes from extrinsic sources such as praise, awards, public recognition, money, power, and those things that tend to corrupt rather than positively empower people. When adversity hits us—and it will, during our lifetime—without passion to do what we have been called to do, we will not get the fulfillment that we all look for, nor will we find an effective solution base to carry on the calling.

Reflecting upon my daily living habits, I have been fortunate to understand what my passion was early, and have tried to convey that passion to positively influence the staff and student athletes that I work with. The internal drive to understand that the Lord has placed me in certain situations to be a witness to his glory and grace continues to assist me in the passion that I approach in my daily living habits. These habits include a daily attempt to provide balance in my life between the spiritual, cognitive, physical, social, and emotional parts of my life; and I make a concentrated effort to portray a passionate reflection on those with whom I have worked closely.

Another critical core value is trustworthiness. Included in this are virtues such as honesty, sincerity, authenticity, and transparency. I believe that with the people in your daily sphere of influence—family, work colleagues, friends—the building of trust becomes critical in providing a foundation where many great things can be accomplished. To achieve this trustworthiness with the people surrounding and exposed to you on a consistent basis, it is first important to reflect upon and evaluate how you have treated those people during your association that day. The Golden Rule (treat others as you would want to be treated) is certainly something I like to keep in front of me. I believe that you should never promise something you cannot deliver (maintaining transparency), and I try to follow that rule with the people who are close to me or in my work environment. Certainly, there are times when I have fallen short, as we all do, but another critical element to building trustworthiness is to admit and take responsibility when you have made a mistake or a bad decision. The innate ability of human beings to forgive, coupled with the sincerity of the admittance when you have made a mistake, goes a long way in mending and building trust amongst family, friends, and coworkers.

The core value of courage is also essential in the field of athletics. I can remember having to play an all-important regional game on the road against a formidable opponent without my two best players, because they were late for the team bus. It was a standard rule that we all followed as a team, and one that had never been tested in my reign until that time. I'm sure the team did not think that I would sit my two best players in this all-important game, but I did, knowing full well we might lose. The lesson I was trying to teach was that there is no one more important than the whole team. Adversity will hit us all in our lifetime, and for one player to think he was more important than the team could not be tolerated—if we, *as a group*, were going to achieve anything.

To our good fortune, we happened to win the game in front of a hostile crowd on a three-point shot with six seconds to go. The two players who were late to the bus were rewarded by sitting next to me on the bench for the entire game. The lesson I learned was that it is critical to exhibit courage and stand by what you have set down in your expectations for anyone you lead, and to hold yourself to the same standards as you do your team members or coworkers.

Finally, I believe it is of utmost importance to have a pure sense of self. One must know who they are and what their strengths are—and be at peace with who they are—in order to lead in any area of life. This is where true leadership begins: in the leading of oneself. This area includes such traits as knowing your sense of purpose, your motivation, and what drives you. To achieve this sense of self, one should obtain as much knowledge as they can. It has been through my experience and biblical divine teaching that this identity of self has evolved for me. I believe that the outgrowth of whatever I am doing should reflect my faith-based belief in Jesus Christ as the Son of God. This reflection does get tarnished at times with my sin nature, but I am always looking to improve my foundational base.

Certainly, there are probably many more core values that could be included. We will touch upon some of them in the following chapters.

A Personal Covenant

What is at your core? This concept is critical if we, as coaches, are to provide the athletes we serve a committed, well-balanced influence in their lives. We have an incredible platform, and it is important for us to recognize the possible impacting influence we have on the people we serve. Often, I have heard the words "role model," and to be honest have not bought into that line of thinking. I personally believe that from our limited human viewpoint, modeling another human being will not address what is needed in our soul—to not only have a competitive nature but also a compassionate one. We as humans have so many limitations that it would be unwise to try and model ourselves on one specific individual. Instead, I believe that we should look to positive influencing factors in our lives that could and probably should come from many individuals. However, at the end of the day, the real model is Jesus Christ himself.

As it has often been said, the basis for leading effectively starts with self. The ability to identify what is at your center, or core, is critical, in the hopes of transferring that to others.

It is important to remember that Jesus came to this earth as a human being. He lived with us for thirty-three years and he experienced all the human emotions that we have. You don't think he was ever disappointed in his team (his disciples)? Ever recall the story of Jesus getting angry in the temple over the money-mongers? Remember the night before he was put to death, realizing Peter would deny him three times. Don't you think it broke his heart, knowing also that one of his own (Judas) would betray him?

What we must remember is that Christ stood for the good—not necessarily the nice. Although he showed an inordinate amount of compassion, humility, and selflessness, don't you think he was highly competitive? He was sent here to give the gospel to mankind and to try and win as many souls for the kingdom as he could. Christ accomplished this by the direct impact he had on his team (disciples) and the people he influenced through his day-to-day interaction. Those who heard him and were in search of a better way to live turned to Christianity, because of Jesus' command and understanding of what his heavenly Father wanted.

In my discussions with other coaches and staff personnel, I am continuously emphasizing that at the level we coach, it is extremely important to understand the normal human's general makeup. Although an athlete's greatest validation is through what they physically achieve, there are several other components that need to be addressed in the hopes of influencing people to become self-sustaining leaders. These human components involve spiritual, cognitive, emotional, and social growth.

It is my belief that the wants and needs of humans, whether young or old, have not changed over the years. The times have changed but athletes are looking for the same types of things in their athletic experience. The need to be directed, guided, disciplined, encouraged, motivated, and valued is still very much a part of what the athlete desires. I have often said there is not one potential student recruit who has sat in my office and not wanted to be successful both as a player and as a human being. The issue becomes, from their perception, what is viewed as being successful. This is a challenge that we face each day in our interactions with our players.

Our goal as Christian coaches is to strive to be Christlike at our core. When we mention something like this, it should be noted we must define what "Christlike" means. My interpretation is that we strive to take on the human characteristics that Jesus had when he was upon this planet earth and incorporate our daily Christian growth to the betterment of our surroundings. A specific example of these traits can be found in Galatians 5:22–23: "But the fruit of the Spirit is love, joy, peace, patience, kindness, goodness, faithfulness, gentleness, and self-control." Those are the core principles we should be trying to promote each day in our lives.

There are several words in this verse that one needs to reflect upon to truly understand. Often, I find that the first characteristic, love, is misinterpreted to mean "being nice," or allowing the player to bend or break the boundaries set because we have a certain affection for the individual. This social-work affection leads us to believe that we can save all the players that we meet, and that therefore as coaches we should try and keep them on our teams at almost any cost. There is a true arrogance in this type of thinking, simply because we cannot be the end-all for every player we have contact with. It also has a selfish connotation to it. To keep someone who is skilled but continually breaks the rules, just for the sake of a few more potential wins, would be an injustice to the other members of the team. If we truly examine the basis for our platform, we can easily deduce this not only is destructive for the individual but can tear apart an entire team. When we allow inappropriate, unethical, or on-the-edge behavior, it gives the player a sense of "this is how it will be once I get into society." In addition, many other individuals are viewing this type of behavioral allowance. It has been my experience that most people will follow what they see, without effectively and efficiently processing whether it is right or wrong. In the case of the highly skilled player, if he/she continues to break rules without consequence, this becomes the norm and others will follow suit.

The act of love is truly a characteristic that takes all the wisdom you have gained from your spiritual growth and life experiences. Our mission is to guide the individual we are coaching to the best of our ability, whether it hurts that individual at the time or not. What we must remember is that if we truly take our platform seriously, immediate gratification will not necessarily be one of the goals. Boundaries are set to empower the receiver (player) to learn difficult lessons and come through them successfully. This could be defined as the impersonal love characteristic of a coach. Many times, we are not able to develop an intimate personal relationship in the short amount of time we are afforded with our players, but we have a true affection for the human condition. Our recognition of the platform we have empowers us with the ability to teach life-skills lessons, as difficult as they may seem.

A simple analogy concerning the social-work affection for someone, which can have a profound outcome, is the rule of being on time to practice. If that is one of your basic rules as a coach and it is continuously broken with no severe consequence, you will have players showing up at all different times, with all kinds of different excuses. Would you be acting out of love for the individual if you allowed this kind of behavior to continue, knowing that later in their lives they would be fired for this kind of insubordination? I think most coaches would say no.

"Joy" is another word that often brings confusion. If we look at this word on the surface, it would appear to mean "continuous happiness." But we all know that is impossible from a human perspective. As we know in the coaching world, there are many different personality types. I may be a generally upbeat person, while other colleagues of mine may possess the melancholy trait, the pessimistic personality, or the realistic trend. The *emotion* of joy would then be impossible for these types to obtain on a consistent basis. However, if we look at this from our spiritual perspective, I believe that what the apostle Paul, the writer of the verse, wants us to know that God is in control from a divine standpoint. If we are maturing as we should in the Word, no matter what the obstacle, our joy is a contentment that all will work out in his plan. This realization brings a balance to our existence, knowing that we have a divine advocate always working for us. This behavior also transfers to the people whom we are coaching, as they observe our demeanor in everyday activities.

Another word that stands out in this biblical verse is "self-control." Self-control recognizes that we all as humans have these negative emotions that are constantly floating around such as envy, anger, jealousy, frustration, and disappointment. It is important for coaches to understand that we need not hide these emotions from our players but use them as teaching tools. Be a witness to the fact that you are not abnormal because these emotions surface—but when they do, teach your players how they may effectively deal with them through the teachings of Scripture. A very positive way to address these negative emotions is to give your players several verses of Scripture they can reach for in times of adversity. Steering them away from the negative, and providing them with a viable tool such as Scripture to deal with adversity, will bring about a discipline and comfort to the individual during times of crisis.

I used to tell my players consistently, "You may not have the physical skill of Michael Jordan, but if you truly love the game as you say you do, you certainly can have the *will* of Michael Jordan." If we truly are Christian coaches striving for spiritual maturity, then we must have the will and drive to learn all we can about the essence of the person of Jesus Christ, and to provide our players effective and efficient ways to deal with adversity, not only within the game they play but in their general life activities.

It Begins in the Center

The principle of centering yourself revolves around balance and identifying what is at your core. In many of us this is a difficult process. It requires one to reflect, evaluate, critically analyze, and think about why we first got into the coaching field, if that has changed over the years, and if so, why. It also requires us to be accountable and responsible for the actions we take, and how those actions may influence or impact others. This is an extremely difficult process, because it forces us to pause. The mere action of reflecting, evaluating, and critically analyzing your own behavior goes against most everything we witness today. Many of us are continuously on the move, with very little time to think about the most important elements in our lives as coaches, and our interactions and relationships with our players. The more one can multitask, the pervasive feeling seems to be, the more efficient one will become. However, to truly understand yourself and feel at peace with who you are, the element of self-reflecting and analyzing is a necessity. It becomes an opportunity to coach yourself and to understand who you are.

I remember, during the journey of completing my doctorate degree, a professor in one of my last classes was always emphasizing not forgetting your personal story. His contention was that your story makes you who you are. Although true, there was something about that concept that seemed to be missing. I would think about all the young men that I had recruited over thirty years of coaching, from all different kinds of backgrounds, and wondered why some seemed to make it in life and some continued to struggle. Often it made no difference what their background and upbringing were; in each case, it seemed to depend on free will and the choices they made. Out of this came the idea that it is extremely important to never forget your personal story because *it is your choices that decide who you become.*

This notion of getting centered and disciplined, identifying the character traits you want to exhibit, allows you to manage and even enhance the world around you—in this case, the young men or women that you are coaching. To do this, we must be as diligent in our spiritual lives as we are in our coaching environment. We must study the Word—not necessarily like a theologian, but we should look to be taught by a pastor-teacher who has some background in Hebrew and Greek for a clearer interpretation of the Bible. In addition, we must be consistent with the way we approach our daily fundamentals of metabolizing the Word and putting into action (daily application) the essence of the Man we are trying to base our core upon.

The Center in Sport as a Core Analogy

With this principle in mind, let us now look at a sports analogy that illustrates how that can benefit the people we are coaching.

Often the center position in basketball is referred to as the post. The offensive perspective of this position allows a team that has a quality post player to go from what a coach would refer to as inside-out. This puts a tremendous amount of pressure on the opposing defense to adjust when the ball goes down to the post or center at the offensive end. I can remember having the pleasure of coaching several NCAA Division I-caliber players who had tremendous offensive skills at the center position. I can remember quite vividly an early season victory midway through my head-coaching career. I sensed that the players were feeling overly good about themselves. This is not necessarily bad, but I felt they were stepping into the area of arrogance both individually and collectively, and that with our level of talent we were not playing to our capacity. The team should have been concentrating on finding the best possible scoring opportunity by going from the inside out, and we were not utilizing that process. In short, we were taking too many perimeter shots.

With that in mind, we had a team meeting, with me leading the discussion. I emphasized that if our returning All-American—who was sixty-two percent from the field, averaging nineteen points a game, but only taking twelve field goal attempts a game—did not receive a touch three out of every four times down the floor in the half-court offensive set, I would replace our perimeter people with players who would get the ball into the post, where he played. To their credit, they were smart enough to understand that going inside presented all sorts of possibilities on the perimeter because our center was also a good passer and unselfish. That team went on to be one of the most successful in the country at that time.

A good defensive center can protect your team's basket. Among those individuals who made a living on their defensive prowess alone were Bill Russell, Dikembe Mutombo, and Ben Wallace. Although their offensive skills were helpful, they literally changed games by protecting their team's basket and covering up for their teammates' mistakes on the perimeter. Offensive players knew they were going to have to earn their points going against those three "in the paint." The result of their individual defense many times led to offense at the other end.

Equating this philosophy to our spiritual life by utilizing the basics of *faith alone in Christ alone* and *growing in the grace and knowledge of our Lord,* we as Christian coaches need to protect our own baskets, so to speak, from harmful distractions and things that sound almost right, but which have flaws that contradict the Word of God. Our spiritual growing process accelerates by learning from a knowledgeable pastor-teacher. This growth allows us to call upon what I refer to as "Stress Relieving Scriptures" (SRS) in times of crisis and challenges. The method of reaching to the Scripture simply means that when we have a distraction that does not feel right to our soul, our defense is to claim a promise (Scripture) from the Bible, which then begins our offense.

I do not have a great memory for Scripture, even though I have spent many years in the church. One of the most effective ways I have found, from my personal experience, was introduced to me years ago by a colleague of mine at the first of the two educational institutions I worked for. I had just become the head basketball coach and athletic director, after sixteen years of being the assistant. One day when I was up in this colleague's office, going over some human resources paperwork, she handed me this tiny, simply decorated rectangular box. I asked her what it was. In a very simple statement she said, "It's a promise box. Believe me, you're going to need it." For the next twenty-three years, that little rectangular box was a part of both offices I occupied. Although not every day, very frequently a Scripture was pulled out of that box over the years.

Examples of these Scriptures that I turn to in times of struggle, challenges, and grief are listed below:

ANGER:

Romans 8:28—And we know that in all things God works for the good of those who love him, who have been called according to his purpose.

Psalm 145:8—The LORD is gracious and compassionate, slow to anger and rich in love.

Proverbs 16:32—Better a patient person than a warrior, one with self-control than one who takes a city.

BELIEF:

Acts 10:43—All the prophets testify about him that everyone who believes in him receives forgiveness of sins through his name.

John 3:18—Whoever believes in him is not condemned, but whoever does not believe stands condemned already because he has not believed in the name of God's one and only Son.

COMFORT:

Psalm 37:24—[T]hough he may stumble, he will not fall.

Psalm 27:14—Wait for the LORD; be strong and take heart and wait for the LORD.

ENDURANCE (Resisting Temptation):

Romans 5:3—Not only so, but we also rejoice in our sufferings, because we know that suffering produces perseverance.

James 1:12—Blessed is the man who perseveres under trial, because, having stood the test, that person will receive the crown of life that the Lord has promised to those who love him.

Hebrews 10:36—You need to persevere so that when you have done the will of God, you will receive what he has promised.

James 1:2–4—Consider it pure joy, my brothers, whenever you face trials of many kinds, because you know that the testing of your faith develops perseverance. Let perseverance finish its work so that you may be mature and complete, not lacking anything.

FEAR:

Isaiah 41:10—So do not fear, for I am with you; do not be dismayed, for I am your God. I will strengthen you and help you; I will uphold you with my righteous right hand.

2 Timothy 1:7—For the Spirit God gave us does not make us timid, but gives us power, love and self-discipline.

1 John 4:18—There is no fear in love. But perfect love drives out fear, because fear has to do with punishment. The one who fears is not made perfect in love.

Psalm 23:1—The LORD is my shepherd, I lack nothing.

Psalm 34:4—I sought the LORD, and he answered me; he delivered me from all my fears.

STRENGTH:

Philippians 4:13—I can do everything through him who gives me strength.

Deuteronomy 31:6—Be strong and courageous. Do not be afraid or terrified because of them, for the LORD your God goes with you; he will never leave or forsake you.

Isaiah 41:10—So do not fear, for I am with you; do not be dismayed, for I am your God. I will strengthen you and help you; yea, I will uphold you with my righteous right hand.

Deuteronomy 20:4—For the LORD your God is the one who goes with you to fight against your enemies to give you victory.

1 Corinthians 10:13—No temptation has overtaken you except what is common to mankind. And God is faithful; he will not let you be tempted beyond what you can bear. But when you are tempted, he will also provide a way out so that you can endure it.

2 Corinthians 12:9—But he said to me, "My grace is sufficient for you, for my power is made perfect in weakness."

I have found that often our misery and hard times are self-induced. In other words, we create the environment we live in by the decisions we make and how we treat the people in our sphere of influence. When misery happens, we ask God to get us out of the situation. He has already given us the tools to pull ourselves out of the muck and mire by going to the above Scriptures, thinking logically how we got ourselves into the predicament in the first place, and evaluating how to get ourselves out. These verses above reflect a divine viewpoint and work for the overall good of the divine plan. They can be used to address certain emotional and mental attitude sins we experience.

This analogy—of the center in basketball to the center of our souls—fits right in with the way that we, as coaches, should view our leadership traits. We coach for the overall good of the team; however, we use the individual talents of everyone to enhance the entire body. The purpose of this type of spiritual drill is to get us to refocus on what is important. It allows us to have a relaxed state of mind, by understanding the challenges that we face and the tools the Word of God has given us. This analogy begins to take meaning by understanding biblical verses and how effectively they can be utilized to keep us grounded in our faith. This method should be part of our core and center.

≫ 3 ≪

BRINGING INFLUENCE ON THE PLATFORM

Let them give glory to the LORD and proclaim his praise in the islands.

— Isaiah 42:12

The field of coaching carries with it the obligation and accountability for all of us to influence the ones we interact with daily. In junior college athletics, you, as coach, are engaged with your athletes for the most part 24/7. You are the person they come to for advice, wisdom, direction, and correction.

The below areas of concentration in your daily living may have a profound effect on the behavior and character development of your players. For at least a short period of time, they will view someone to model their daily living habits after—and as a result, hopefully continue to grow their own sense of value and behavioral traits.

Balance

Balance is the conscious act of not overextending ourselves, let alone to a point of extreme indulgence. When we speak of this in physical terms, it means not too far to the left, right, forward, or backward. The better athlete has a good sense of balance, and actually practices fundamental drills that will help improve balance.

This is an extremely delicate area when we speak in terms of being a coach, because one's human nature almost always turns to the object of their passion. However, let us think of this in the terms of our Christian nature and the fact that Jesus Christ is the Son of God, to whom all our sins are imputed by his sacrifice on the cross. Our call begins with *faith alone in Christ alone*. As stated in John 5:24, Jesus said, "Very truly I tell you, whoever hears my word and believes him who sent me has eternal life and will not be judged but has crossed over from death to life." What a great promise by the divine heavenly Father. This means that once we have committed, we have crossed over; no matter how many human mistakes we make, our salvation is secure. Secondly, once we have committed, we are mandated to *grow in grace and knowledge of our Lord and Savior Jesus Christ* (2 Pet. 3:18).

The point that I am trying to make is that I believe salvation is simple, just as coaching is simple. In religion (not true Christianity), man is continuously trying to fix things himself and create all kinds of "building blocks" to get to heaven through the "good works" philosophy. As you think about that, one should ask the question: When is enough good stuff I do *enough*?

The same goes in the coaching field. It is simple in nature and we tend to overcomplicate the process. When is enough game film *enough*? When is enough scouting *enough*? When are enough late-night talks about personnel *enough*?

Go back to our two Scriptures above. Consider our mandates as believers in Jesus the Son of God, then think about this: If a player *believes* in you as his/her coach, and decides to *grow* in the knowledge you are giving him or her, he or she will have a successful athletic life.

Analogies comparing the coaching/athletic journey to the spiritual journey are common. As we grow and mature in our knowledge by studying the Word, I believe our coaching expertise (not necessarily in the Xs and Os of the game) grows relationally with our players because of our foundational base and centered core. Players find a security and peace of their own when they have a coach who has consistency and direction both in their coaching and behavior. The coach begins to understand that if we truly want the opportunity to witness through our actions, the Word gives us many avenues.

Not long ago, I received a call from one of my former players, who had been a starter on one of our NJCAA Region 4 championship teams. He had gone on to an NCAA Division 2 school on a full scholarship, completed his degree, and went on to receive his master's in business administration. At our last conversation, he was working for a large insurance company as a regional manager, training salespeople who aspire to be managers. During our discussion, he reflected on our two years together and stated that there was one thing that always stood out in his mind. He recalled how I continued to emphasize that as a human being you never stay the same; whether it is in your spiritual, personal, physical, or professional life, you either mature, or you revert to old bad habits. We referred to this effort to continually grow as "Rise and Grind."

If you want a chance to realize your dream, you need to be willing to "Rise and Grind"—no matter if it is in your personal, professional, academic, or athletic experience. People who are willing to go the journey and display resiliency are usually the ones who end up being successful. This is the way it should be in our spiritual growth. I have fallen short many times in this spiritual endeavor, but I have always found I am more at peace with myself when I have pursued the spiritual side in my day-to-day living.

The point is: In any balancing act, we should start with ourselves. It is difficult to project balance to others unless you are striving in that direction.

Leading with Integrity

Simply put, this is purity of intent in our coaching experience—doing things for the right reasons, and for the good. This coincides with our both our spiritual journey and the journey of coaching our players and coworkers.

There are several leadership qualities we can build along our journey of coaching that will help us develop into the witnesses, and more comprehensive coaches, we can be in the field of athletics. The following traits I believe will empower not only the leader (coach) but also the followers, as they observe the way their coach evaluates, deliberates, collaborates, cooperates, motivates, and disciplines with a consistent, even demeanor. These traits are as follows: knowledge, maturity, flexibility, endurance, assertiveness, compassion, poise, decisiveness, sense of humor, humility, competitive spirit, and accountability. Let's briefly discuss each of these traits as they relate to building the holistic coach, and making that splash you are looking for with your athletes.

Thirst for Knowledge

By "thirst for knowledge," I am talking about understanding what the job entails. This area should be a given. However, in many cases, the coach may have knowledge of the sport, but the transference of that knowledge to the player gets lost because the method of transferring it is not effective.

Let's get this straight: We all make mistakes, no matter how much knowledge we obtain. We will never be perfect in our interpretation or knowledge base, no matter how hard we try. As you think about this, reflect upon the way many young athletes are brought up in their sport. The fact is that in many cases when they get to our level (college), they have become good in only one aspect of their skill: their athleticism. The player has been so much more athletic than their counterparts at the lower levels that it is difficult to discipline them in the very foundation or basics of the game, along with teaching the mental aspect of the sport they are playing.

When I was growing up, in many cases there were maybe three to five different drills to teach the same principle or foundational base. Since the basis of my career was in basketball, a simple example of a foundational base would be how to pass the ball to the post and not have it stolen. We had two drills that taught us that foundation and that was it.

Today's athlete is inundated with multiple ways of getting the same thing done, which means that they are coming from an environment that is constantly stimulating them. Thus, our coaching takes on a more comprehensive approach as we look for ways to keep our athletes' attention with different drills. This type of teaching takes time and effort, which coaches will often not put in because it is tedious work. The result: The athletes' accountability is compromised, because they do not have the foundational skills to be held accountable to. If we are going to teach accountability and responsibility to our athletes, we need to not only educate them but continuously reinforce the appropriate way to do things.

As we know, knowledge can be obtained in many ways. Certainly, through our reading we obtain knowledge that helps us with the fundamental aspects of the game. However, it is important for the coach to also go to workshops, seminars, and networking events to continuously try to grow and mature in his/her profession. No matter what age you are, a coach who does not continue to seek out avenues to grow is a coach who is digressing. One item of importance in today's world, for example, is identifying the consistent methods of communication that our young people are using, and to educate them on the "good" and "bad" forms of social media that are out there. If you want to be an effective communicator, you must jump into some of their world to achieve this.

I have found it very interesting to read about leaders. Effective and efficient behavioral trends transcend across different professions. Any sport in each of our areas of expertise must be taken in and mentally digested for it to become a part of who we are as coaches. This may take years. Leadership philosophies are consistently an evolving process. However, do not make the mistake of the old saying, "practice makes perfect." Practice makes *permanent*! If I am practicing in the wrong way I will continue to do things incorrectly.

In addition, we must learn how important it is to continue to grow in our relational knowledge with our players. Academic knowledge (the Xs and Os, drills, etc.) is one thing, but the ability to motivate, inspire, and promote the "all-in" attitude is another. It has been my experience, through observing, researching, and educating the generation that is upon us, that they relish a more intimate relationship with the coach—a relationship built upon mutual trust and respect. To learn about this important dynamic of interpersonal leading is as critical to our coaching success as the academic knowledge. In today's world of athletics, relational knowledge may be *more* important than the Xs and Os. Learning how to motivate, inspire, and even change the way our athletes deal with both success and failure—so it becomes a way of life—is an obligation our platform affords us.

This can also be said of our spiritual growth. If we elevate good works and being a good moral person above the biblical mandate of growing in the grace and knowledge of our Lord, we are practicing the foundational base incorrectly. Good works for divine cause and being a good moral person may be outgrowths of growing in the grace and knowledge of our Lord, but they should not supersede our biblical mandates.

Our Christian platform also revolves around this philosophy. Knowledge for knowledge's sake is not good. The academic knowledge we learn through the right pastor (coach) who feeds us with the truth must be metabolized, just as if we were eating food that energizes the physical body. By metabolizing the truth, we have an automatic filtering system that empowers the Christian coach to effectively sift through the distractions of the worldly view and focus on the more divine aspects of their souls.

Maturity

As our growth in the Christian faith and our core develops, the maturity level of our decision-making process begins to take shape. Our ability to make wise decisions, eliciting confidence in judgment and integrity, allows us to tackle the difficult process of identifying the personnel who are best suited for the good of the team. This is a critical quality of a leader. The leader (coach) must view what is best from the global approach, in order for a group to function as a cohesive unit or body. Each player has certain gifts he/she brings to the table, and it is our job to bring those gifts out. One of the elements of a mature decision maker is that the leader almost never takes an instantaneous reactive approach to their decision making. We should never make a major decision during the heat of the moment, but must give ourselves time to recover and refuel before making a tough decision.

Early in my head-coaching career, I faced one of these challenges, as my team was struggling through a very tough period. They were mired in a slump with a below .500 record, morale was low, and they began to question themselves and the system. I had several discussions with my coaching staff and numerous sleepless nights, wrestling with the right thing to do for the group. After quite a bit of reflection, I decided to sever ties with one of my better players. There were several factors involved in this decision, but the overwhelming one was his lack of acceptance of my authority as his leader. The ability to take constructive criticism without rebuttal was just not in his DNA, at least not with me. He was always challenging and questioning the overall scheme of what we were doing. I decided I was not the right teacher for him and that another place would fit him better. We were going to move forward without him.

Amazingly, after trying to go forward without this player and suffering through three straight losses, our team began to form their own identity—accepting their roles, sharing the ball, gang rebounding, diving for loose balls, and executing both offensively and defensively with more precision. It was as if all the members were functioning as one body, and it was a wonderful sight to see. The team proceeded to win nine of their last eleven games, and an NJCAA Region 4 title.

As I reflected upon the above story, the transformation of the team reminded me of 1 Corinthians 12:12, as the apostle Paul wrote about the unity and diversity of the body of Christ: "Just as a body, though one, has many parts, but all its many parts form one body, so it is with Christ." That difficult decision allowed a struggling team to blossom and realize their full capacity as a functioning unit. Little did I know at the time that the great apostle Paul had written about that very concept almost two thousand years earlier.

We, as Christians, are the functioning body of Christ on this earth. Each of us has spiritual gifts we can give to that endeavor to work for the overall good. Our witness can take many forms such as action, exhortation, servant leading, witnessing, helps, and pastoring-teaching, to name a few. As it is with athletes, there are some who have the "total package," while some are limited to a certain gift that stands out. As I have told my players many times, you are obligated to use whatever your physical gift may be for the overall good of the body. The same can be said for us as Christian coaches. Use of our spiritual gifts is an obligation we must utilize.

Flexibility

Not all people are motivated or inspired in the same way. Many times, bringing our influence requires a paradigm shift. Often we are rigid in our approach to leading, and as a result may miss the opportunity to affect someone for the good. Good coaching and good leading is about relationships, looking for ways to not lose your own core and set of values, and at the same time search for ways to teach the same values from a different point.

This may have been the most difficult part of coaching for me. I was brought up by coaches who had a certain set of criteria and rules that everyone had to follow, no matter who you were. Lost in that rigidity of thinking is the fact that there are different ways to motivate and guide people into doing what you want done.

Flexibility allows the coach to make timely and appropriate change for the good of the group. Coaches must get away from being always predictable in their approach. That does not mean you do not have boundaries and consequences. It does mean that you share, dialogue, and get to know your players, finding out what motivates them and how you can help them feel valued without sacrificing your core principles.

Do not feel that your leadership is threatened in any way if you have an "ear" to your followers. Listen or you will become detached and out of touch. Not listening leads to conflict and loss of leadership in your coaching style.

Endurance

Endurance is the willingness to "go the distance." Anything worth having in this life is about the failures, rewards, successes, disappointments, and all the other factors that encompass our travel.

Any long and short-term goals set are going to require a journey, with many variables to achieve. We all know about this—how long the journey takes and the peaks and valleys that the coach and athlete go through during a season. People remember John Wooden's hall-of-fame journey with the UCLA Bruins. What they do not remember is that he did not win his first championship until fifteen years after he accepted the position. In addition, he was always refining his "pyramid of success" as an ever-evolving leadership paradigm.

I have always equated the athletic journey with a visual of the Rocky Mountains. We all begin on this level ground (ground zero); and once our vision (what do we want to do) and mission (how are we going to get there) have been set, we begin our trip to hopefully the highest peak. At our level, it was the National Junior College Athletic Association Finals. Along our journey, we are often climbing and making progress up the slope, but because of a variety of circumstances we get knocked down a level—not back to ground zero, but somewhere in between. At that point, we pause and evaluate what we did wrong, then proceed up the slope again with a new resolve. This can happen many times during a season, and many times we do not achieve our goals, but we learn many things along the way that keep us going and wanting more. We continue to battle for what we believe!

As Christian coaches striving to live the spiritual life, we encounter similar adversities in our tendencies to embrace the world's view on ideas and theories, rather than exercising our rights as Christians and going to the divine view in prayer. This happens repeatedly as the spiritual battle wages on in us. We seem to be making progress, and then something unforeseen or unpredictable shakes our faith somewhat. We pause, evaluate, refuel with prayer and meditation, and continue up the slope to spiritual maturity. It is important to understand that with our spiritual maturity we are equipped with the tools to better weather these storms, and to show a certain amount of graciousness as we endure.

Assertiveness

Functioning under the premise that many people are followers, it is important for any coach to be assertive in his/her leadership. There is this theory that floats around concerning athletes and their leadership abilities transferring to others; that is not necessarily true. I believe that given our coaching platform, our priority is to try and empower the athlete to be able to lead his or herself. That specific function is so important to understand, because many of us do not want or have the desire to lead others. If the athlete wants and has the capacity to lead, that trait should be recognized by the coach. Someone who can take charge when necessary, justly and appropriately, without overexcess of emotion or anger, has more of an opportunity to win the followers' loyalty. The leader will provide the follower with a "buy-in" to the vision we want from our teams. Players with positive volition (attitude) will respond to this.

Compassion

Compassion is the ability to be sensitive to the individual feelings of someone, relative to the group. The capacity to exhibit this characteristic in your coaching platform empowers the coach to become more personal and intimate with the players. In a study that I did with 145 athletes, one of the pervasive themes that came out as I interviewed them is that they wanted a more personal relationship with the coach. Often these young athletes are treated as commodities for much of their lives, and the elite ones are viewed many times as a business investment. What is forgotten in this scenario is that these are young human beings who are being shaped to react to the world around them. If the only experience they have is being rewarded for their physical gift, their world becomes distorted; they only have the capacity to interact and feel most comfortable on the field of competition.

In a commercial I saw recently during the NCAA Men's Basketball Tournament, it was revealed that there were approximately 480,000 college athletes, and that only two percent would earn their living through their respective sports. That statement would mean, in pure numbers, there would be about 470,400 doing something else. When that world collapses around them (and it does eventually), those athletes who did not go on professionally in their sport are left with very few life skills. In showing compassion—and by searching for different avenues to redirect, motivate, and guide your players into other, more realistic visions—the coach becomes more than a coach. Words such as leader, teacher, mentor, and counselor begin to emerge when the relationship goes beyond the field of competition.

Poise

My definition of poise is the ability to maintain on-task focus relative to the mission at hand, even when everything going on around you is chaotic. The simple task of playing a competitive basketball game has many adverse situations that present themselves during a contest. It is a roller-coaster of emotional outlet. As a coach, the capacity to have confident control of emotions under adverse situations puts your players more at ease, and allows them to grow in this area.

Decisiveness

This characteristic is so critical in the development of our platform that it is often overlooked, because of the sometimes-confrontational consequences that may arise. A coach who can make quick, firm, and clear decisions in a game or in personnel decisions gains the overall respect of the entire group. This takes an incredible amount of maturity on the part of the coach, and often it becomes on-the-job training. In the end, one must look at what is best for the team and move on from that point.

Many times, in the course of decision-making, an ethical challenge raises its ugly head. Therefore, it is not only important to know what the right decision is, but to have the moral courage to do the right thing.

Humor

The ability to laugh at your own mistakes and shortcomings gives the player a sense of your human side. This characteristic can often diffuse conflict, anxiousness, or anxiety. We all have shortcomings, and it is important to remember that.

The subject of humor reminds me of our team in the 1999–2000 season. We were fortunate to have one of the best teams in the country at our level and to make it to the Final Four of the NJCAA Tournament. That year, we had certain rituals we followed before we took the court, as taught to me by my mentor. In this instance, we were playing in front of approximately eight thousand people and the atmosphere was electric. I had always prided myself in being totally focused on the task at hand, and had conveyed that to all my players during the season. Our normal locker-room ritual was to go over our offensive and defensive game plan, along with player defensive assignments, any last-minute discussion, and motivational applications. After this part of the pregame, we would all gather in a circle with hands held and take a moment of silence. All my players knew I was a Christian man, so I would say a prayer thanking God for the opportunity to be in the moment, asking that no one would be seriously injured and to play our competitive best.

However, on this night (and after what I thought was a rousing motivational speech), I encouraged the team and headed out the tunnel. No one followed me, and I heard one of my sophomores say, "Hey coach, you scared?" I looked back and realized the circle had formed without me in it. I had lost my focus, as we would say.

I came back to the circle, grabbed hands on both sides of me, and said, "You're damn right I'm scared." Everyone got a good laugh, easing the tension of the moment, and we had our ten seconds of silence, thanking the Lord for the opportunity we had in front of us.

Humility

My definition of humility is the sincere capacity to recognize the resources (both organizational and human) that allowed you to get to the point of success, and to make sure those resources are appropriately appreciated. My father used to always say to me, "Be careful how you treat people on the way up because you will meet them again on the way back down." The lesson is that although professional success is an enjoyable state of mind, it is temporary for most of us; and that respect, courtesy, and civility go a long way in the positive influence of others. Another way to look at this is remembering the phrase "Success is fleeting, but relationships last a lifetime."

We are not born with humility; it is something that is learned from a young age and needs to be nurtured. Often, we are so engrossed in building up the young person to have confidence that we tend to go overboard, and in the end, give the individual a sense of entitlement. We reward them for the simplest accomplishments. This type of system creates individuals who have extreme challenges in dealing with adversity, because their entire life has been one of rewards. As coaches, it is our obligation from a holistic sense to provide our athletes with the tools to deal with success and adversity in a balanced way. Simply put, humility is the ability not to think less of yourself but to think of yourself less often.

Competitive Spirit

When people discuss the person of Jesus Christ, I cannot remember ever hearing anyone referring to his great competitive spirit! Yet from my point of view, he was the greatest competitor of all time. Where most of us are trying to win the next contest, Christ was trying to win souls for the eternal future of mankind. He was totally devoted to the task and was all about empowering his team (disciples) to carry on the journey until his reappearance. As Christian men and women coaches, it is our obligation to carry on as witnesses to our faith.

When one looks at the above characteristics that we can bring to the table as coaching leaders, it should be noticed the enormous responsibility the platform demands. However, if we have "both feet in," as we would want our athletes to, we exhibit that the journey is not only doable but enjoyable and exciting!

Accountability

You will make mistakes. The ability to own up to these miscues, no matter what the consequences, will increase your growth and understanding of the gravity of your platform. This particular trait was severely tested when I changed jobs in the mid-2000s. I had been employed as an athletic director at a two-year school in South Florida. I had always prided myself in following the rules—specifically, in this case, with compliance and athletic eligibility. In this situation, on my first year on the job, I had not educated myself well enough and had overextended our scholarship offerings in a certain sport. Upon finding this out, I immediately self-reported. The result is that we lost three full scholarships for that year. It was truly a humbling experience, and one I paid attention to for the rest of my professional career.

The above individual characteristics are of critical importance to the leader, but just as important is the way that they are incorporated within the process of the group. The following group core values should be continually nurtured throughout the season.

Trustworthiness

Development of trust from coach to coach, coach to player, and player to player is of utmost importance in the creation of an environment that has success. The sense of open and honest communication with all in your sphere of influence will mature and enhance relationships with the people with whom you work on a day-to-day basis. Integrity, along with competence, go a long way in developing an environment of trustworthiness. It is important to admit when you make mistakes and to remain accountable for what you do. As the leader, however, it is important that your people have the perception that you have the knowledge base and competence to lead in your area of expertise. Nurturing values such honesty, authenticity, and being forthcoming and transparent go a long way in developing this group trait.

Valuing People

Leaders who serve have a good grasp of one of the basic characteristics of leadership—and that is, to empower your people. This allows the leader to understand that the players, assistant coaches, and support people who have been provided within the work environment are the greatest resources that a leader can have. It is important to understand that looking and searching for ways to maximize the meaning of the work relationship and environment provides an environment for continuous quality improvement. The understanding that your athletic group is most likely a subculture of a more global culture brings the leader to look for the best ways to collaborate and celebrate successes that are truly organizationally based. This willingness to empower the athlete and your colleagues gives them an opportunity to invest in the healthy culture you are creating.

Creating an Environment for Successful Sustainability

This one is possibly the least-thought-about group value, because it takes a combination of personal humility and passion. "What will happen when I leave?" should be a question that all leaders ask. If they are true servants to the leadership community, they will want things to successfully progress as if they were not even there. The truly successful leader will understand the importance of empowering the people in your leadership community, and of utilizing the diversity of talents that are available.

Whether it is leading an entire organization, a division within that organization, a community service project, an athletic team or a personal family issue, the passion with which one approaches their leadership, along with a sense of humility, creates this sustainable environment. Although the cultural climate we find ourselves in as coaches may not be conducive to creating this sustainability, it is our obligation to try to encourage this value. In addition, an outgrowth of this sustainable environment would be to have a mentoring program, allowing leaders of the community to provide training in areas that will enable this environment to be successfully carried on.

Open Dialogue and the Free Flow of Ideas

Even in a healthy, functioning community of leadership, this preferred group value takes a sense of courage. The engagement of players and staff emphasizing the encouragement of ideas and thoughts, even debate, often tends to be intimidating to the leader. This process does at times become tedious and time-consuming; however, the rewards can be extremely beneficial if used in the right way. This process allows the diversity of talents to be realized, and for everyone to feel an actual ownership of the athletic program. This sharing of ideas can be embraced as not necessarily good for everyone each time, but what is just, fair, and good for the group.

As we create an environment for healthy interaction, it is important to integrate your individual characteristics for the good of the group. It has been noted that balance in your life is extremely critical to this process. By creating a balanced perspective in your own day-to-day actions, you can then project this balance to others.

In addition, as you work on your individual characteristics, these attributes will be recognized by others within your sphere of influence—translating them into the corporate core values you would like from within the group. All three of these areas—balance in your personal life, individual leadership characteristics, and corporate core values for a healthy competitive culture—will enable you to lead with integrity, and with purity of intent.

In the end, bringing a positive influence to our platform is what we should be striving for in our athletic culture—or, for that matter, any culture we impact.

≫ 4 ≪

THE POWER OF HUMILITY

Do nothing out of selfish ambition or vain conceit.
Rather in humility others better than yourselves.

— Philippians 2:3

Humility is one of the most powerful characteristics a successful human being can have. I have been taught many lessons in humility over the years, but the most prominent is not even related to the sport world. It was given to me by a calico cat named Wednesday.

Approximately fourteen years ago, on a Labor Day weekend of 2003, I was introduced to a ten-pound ball of fur that forever changed my way of thinking on humility. I was becoming acquainted with a new friend (my future wife) in her home; and as we talked, these small heads peeked out from behind the hallway wall. They were all shapes and colors and, as this breed of animal usually is, they were inquisitive. I asked my new friend how many of these creatures she had; she replied, "Seven." Seeing only six at the time, I didn't question any further.

We continued to converse for some time and then, as I got up to leave, I saw this small creature sitting on top of a reclining chair, gazing at the wood-burning fire in another one of the rooms—oblivious to, and showing no interest in, the new visitor in the house. That was my first experience with this Snickers-Bar-looking cat with black, brown, and white fur; coal-black eyes; and golden slits.

I have always liked animals. Through my upbringing, I have believed they were put on earth for a specific reason. But this relationship became so much more incredible because of what it taught me. As the relationship with my future wife progressed during the years, my relationship with Wednesday basically remained the same. She had enough attention from my future wife and her children, so I would just stroke her fur from time to time and enjoy watching her.

All of that changed six years ago. My wife and I had been married for a year, and we decided to transport Wednesday down with us to Florida where I was currently working. Although two of our children were taking care of Wednesday in Illinois, my wife and I decided that Wednesday would be a good addition, and she became a permanent resident with us.

Wednesday had been rescued by my wife some fourteen years earlier; so in cat age, she was getting old. In any case, we became friends and loved our daily routine of getting up at 5 a.m. for her feeding, watering, and hanging out in front of the TV for the local news or Sports Center before I was off to work. And when I came home from work, it was the same routine. Not long after that move we noticed that Wednesday was having issues jumping, walking, being able to go to the bathroom, and other ailments. We took her to the vet several times and a myriad of problems popped up that indicated she was eventually going to leave us soon: an enlarged heart, signs of kidney failure, severely arthritic hind legs, and a highly congested bowel tract.

During those failing times, you would never know she was going through extreme pain.

When she sat down at my feet each night, she would spend significant time just sitting and purring while, I'm sure now, she was in extreme pain. When we picked her up in the bed with us, she would just purr to let us know she was right there with us.

As I was sitting one night, close to the end, I must have looked at that tiny, defenseless, always-willing-to-please creature for an hour and thought to myself about the great capacity the love of my Lord has for us humans. In his all-powerful and perfect wisdom, he brought us a visual sign through our pets, to remind us daily of how selfless, compassionate, tender, caring, and willing to please they are, and of how totally dependent and trusting they are, no matter how broken or flawed we may be. God knew that going to him in meditation, fellowship, and prayer may not be enough all the time, because we live in faith. Thus, he created these visual models for us. Wednesday was a supreme comforter with no other agenda other than to make her owners happy; in turn, that made her happy. As her little chest grabbed for air in those final hours and we put her humanely down, I watched the life go out of her eyes, lying on her favorite blanket, at 12:42 p.m. on Friday, September 18, 2015. I wept.

At that moment, Wednesday also taught me one deeper spiritual revelation about humility: The humblest sacrifice of all was from the all-righteous, all-powerful creator of all things, God our Father. He in his humility saw how broken we were as human beings; and instead of just abandoning the project, he gave us his uniquely born Son to give us a chance at an eternity with him. We as humans many times cannot even comprehend divine humility, so God gives us—even for maybe just a short time—creatures like our pets to provide visual reinforcement of his love and grace. This memory has often reminded me of the following verse:

> I also said to myself, "As for humans, God tests them so that they may see that they are like the animals. Surely the fate of human beings is like that of the

animals; the same fate awaits them both: As one dies, so dies the other. All have the same breath; humans have no advantage over animals. Everything is meaningless. All go to the same place; all come from dust, and to dust all return. Who knows if the human spirit rises upward and if the spirit of the animal goes down into the earth? (Eccl. 3:18–21)

I remember, early in my head-coaching career, entering the regional tournament with a team that was average on pure physical ability but overachieving. I thought I had made all the right moves during the season, and that we were going into the tournament—possibly overmatched in talent, but playing as well as we had all season.

During that three-game span to win our tenth regional title in the school's history (our first with me at the helm), we had defeated two of the top twenty-five ranked teams in the country. This was my first title as head coach, and at forty-two years young I was feeling full of myself. To put this in perspective, the National Tournament was now pared down from two hundred twenty-six to twenty-four. With one more win, we would be part of the "Sweet 16" for the sixth time in the history of the school.

As we took the long bus trip down to Southern Illinois to play in the interregional game, I felt we had a great shot to play well and win. The trip went well, the confidence was high, and the game plan was meticulously laid out. As we began the game, we ran a set play off the tip, scored on a three-point basket, and we were on our way—or so I thought. Mysteriously, at that moment the shot clock malfunctioned and there was a twenty-minute delay. The momentum from our good start had been taken away. When the game proceeded, our opponent went on a 22-0 run, which we never recovered from. Final score, opponent 83, to our 52!

As I was slowly walking to the locker room (all by myself, I might add), I smiled. Having been a preacher's kid and a Christian for the longest time, I always thought I had the Lord right beside me and within me—which we do. Often it is he who gets you in check with your own arrogance and egocentric behavior. So, as I smiled and spoke aloud, I said, "Lord, you made your point." This is what I refer to as divine forced humility—being brought to a state where you understand that, without the instruments or tools placed in front of you to achieve, you would have no success at all.

Humility is not an innate characteristic. It is not in our DNA when we are born. It must be learned. We learn humility through guidance, direction, correction, and discipline as we are growing up and through life's lessons. This process must be started early in our young people, through the enforcement of correction, motivation, and guidance. These above processes should not be confused with awarding our young children for simply participating and being engaged in extracurricular activities. Rewards for doing these types of things provide a false sense of importance and worth. In some people's thinking this philosophy may sound cruel, but if you love someone and are invested in their well-being there must be adversity, and sometimes unfair authority, for growth to take place. If we do not teach our young people how to be resilient during adverse times, we are doing them a disservice.

There were many times during my coaching career when we won basketball games and yet did not play up to our capabilities. If you have ever coached, this is always a concern. In a coach's mind, knowing that each game is a different journey, you fear that players will accept that kind of performance moving forward. Often in those instances, besides discussing this in the walls of our locker room, we would then take it out to the floor for a practice right after the game. This was not a punishment type of practice with suicide drills or wind sprints; it was an actual practice where we addressed issues such as effort, execution, defensive transition, and other areas where we had fallen short during that game. Most importantly, I did not want to let a teaching moment pass us by. Much of the application in coaching is not only by seeing and hearing but by actual doing.

In this world of entitlement and immediate gratification, we as coaches need to continue to reinforce and teach the aspect of humility to our young people. As I reflect on this, I think again about the simple yet profound tool God had presented to mature my thinking on the aspect of humility: Wednesday the Snickers-Bar-looking cat!

≫ 5 ≪

PURPOSE AND PASSION

*Listen to advice and accept instruction, and in the
end, you will be wise.*

— Proverbs 19:20

A Boundless Enthusiasm

As an outgrowth of our faith-based principles, I will try to crystallize and define several areas of our life that allow us to obtain a better balance. Our individual characteristics, and the things we hold dear to us, will begin to blossom and the players that we coach will notice. One of those characteristics will be passion. Our willingness to learn about the person of Christ will in turn intensify and bring into focus our human passion for what we do in relationship to our professional love of sport.

I can remember that when I was in my youth and beginning to learn the game of basketball, I was always trying to find a way to play. Growing up in the Midwest, the outside elements were often not conducive to playing, but that never stopped me. I would shovel the snow off the driveway, or use salt to de-ice that small rectangular half court, so I could shoot. Often it was just too cold on my hands, so I purchased these thin gloves that formed to my fingers and it worked out just fine. As with all youngsters, net or no net on the rim, I was going to play. In the summer heat, I would take a sack lunch to the local grade school and practice my shooting and defensive fundamentals, and in the evening go to the park and play pickup games. When I saw someone who had gifted skills but didn't take the time to nurture them, I thought what a waste it was.

As I grew older and tried to develop my skills to compete in the game I loved, I noticed my human tendency to take it easy. Often, I found I needed a coach. Because of many committed and well-educated men who knew the game of basketball, I would develop into an effective and efficient part of a team. I was one of the primary producers offensively in high school, junior college, and four-year college. My sincere love for the game grew. I was not only going through the process of developing my physical skills; I was also studying the game from a cognitive (mental) aspect. This early development assisted me greatly, as I stepped into coaching back in 1977. I also began to take notice of the support from people around me and how they guided, motivated, and directed me (although at times I didn't like it).

During my playing career, one of the distinct memories I have is of my father. As I reflect on our relationship, I understand how truly fortunate I was to have a male figure consistently in my life. It wasn't necessarily the verbal dialogue and sitdown talks we had, because they were very rare; it was his actions that had such an impact on me. He never missed a game. He even made the away games. At one time in my college career I counted how many games he was not able to make from junior high through college—he missed two games. This is my most vivid recollection of a father who had passion for his son.

Often in today's world, we see many parents trying to live out their own frustrated sports lives through their children. They are highly vocal, and many times inappropriate with their behavior. This was not my father. The great characteristics I noticed about him during that entire time were his devotion, loyalty, and passion for his son without interference—meaning that he would never interfere or talk negative about the coach, and would not offer advice other than, "You need to do what the coach tells you and work harder."

One specific time I remember was when I transferred from the local junior college to a small four-year school in the northwest suburbs of Chicago. I was a highly touted (or so I thought) JUCO all-state player and all-conference first team. I had interest from some larger colleges and universities, but I was smart enough to know that at 5 feet 8 inches tall, 150 pounds dripping wet, and not excitingly quick (aside from my shot preparation and release), I would be best suited for a small college where I could play immediately. To my amazement, I was beaten out for a starting guard position—by a freshman! Here I was, a junior in college, and since I began playing organized basketball in fifth grade I was always a starter! Talk about a humbling experience.

At the tender age of twenty, this was one of the most difficult experiences of my life, but my father never wavered. His passion for his son continued to shine forward, as he would not miss a game. His simple advice to me was, "If you want this badly enough, earn the position back" (which I eventually did).

This devotion, loyalty, and passion for his son carried over into my coaching career, as he continued to attend games and support me throughout my career. He did change somewhat, as fathers with wisdom will do; he began coaching me on how to coach my players. Now that my dad has passed away, I smile when I recall our "talks" after some of those games.

What Is Passion?

Passion can have many different connotations. We do know that it is a powerful emotion that encompasses both positive and negative outlets. The definition that I like of "passion" comes from Webster's: "the boundless enthusiasm for the object of one's affection." "Boundless" means there are no limitations, so learn all you can, with unadulterated enthusiasm, about the object of your affection.

The great part about passion is that you can develop many passions within your sphere and have a positive influence on the people in your circle. In the first chapter, we talked about the core; this passion goes back to your faith-based principles as coaches of a Christian faith. Remember, the outgrowth and transference of anything we do is based upon what is at our core, our center. Are we as enthusiastic and boundless about our spiritual maturity and study of the Word of God as we are about coaching? I ask myself this question many times, and have always fallen short.

Development of this passion takes work. I often think and relate everything back to myself. In my human and imperfect way, many times in my coaching career I would try to fix things myself. This resulted in extra time in the office coordinating game film, searching for solutions to personnel issues, preparing game plans against the next opponent, worrying about how our recruiting efforts were going, and the myriad of things coaches worry about.

As Christian coaches, it is our place to understand our purpose, and that we cannot permanently fix what attitudes, views, and lifestyles young people are acclimated to. The only way people change is first, if they want to, and second, by the willingness to take instruction and advice. Therefore, the passion of your core faith-based principles must be at work. We need to understand that the human aspects of what we do every day can be so much more enhanced by the spiritual diligence we show to the person of Christ.

I would say to all coaches out there who are men and women of Christian faith that integrating spiritual growth into your life will elevate not only your passion for coaching, but it will result having passion for your quality of life and in your personal relations.

Remember our definition of "passion": the capacity of boundless enthusiasm, immersing ourselves into the object of our affection. Our application to revealing our passion can take many forms. It is important to remember that our definition includes the word "enthusiasm." This emotion has so many positive connotations. When we think of a person who is enthusiastic, we think of an individual who is completely immersed in his or her field of interest—music, art, sports, math, research, the list goes on.

I have often heard—and I subscribed to this, at one time—that the field of coaching takes so much out of you, if you are truly passionate about it, it is hard to develop anything else in your life. I used that same philosophy as a crutch in my own life. I would rationalize that the reason I have gone through divorce is that I couldn't balance my life and that coaching took too much out of me. Baloney! The truth of the matter is not that I couldn't develop anything else in my life; I simply chose not to. Thus, things that should have been important to me (my relationship with God and my family) suffered. I talked the talk (i.e., God first, family second, and all other things below) but I certainly did not walk the walk, and still at times make that mistake repeatedly. Simply put, it is my own arrogance that suggests that I alone can fix it all. I continually find that without the indwelling of Jesus Christ, fixing things is an impossible task. However, with all those personal mistakes, the Lord sent me a beautiful Christian woman who has the capacity to show me all the things I strive for, through her own life.

One of the most basic elements to showing our purpose and passion in the coaching field is how we manage our time. We as coaches are always stressing the importance of time management to our players, yet in our own lives we seem to forget about it.

I can remember sitting down with my team each year, before the season started after we had classes scheduled. We would have a session where we taught everyone how to plan their day with regard to class, study, and practice. In addition, we would incorporate our game schedule into the plan, with school breaks and such, so on a week-by-week basis the players could view what they should be doing at certain times not only during the day but throughout the semester. I would also do the same with my coaching staff in relation to recruiting, practice plan, offensive and defensive breakdown drills, personnel and in what positions they were most effective, and a myriad of other basketball-related items. These activities were an application outgrowth of the game that we all loved and had a passion about. It also showed these athletes that we were concerned on a personal level about how they organized and disciplined themselves in their own lives, in the hopes they would embrace some of these ideals.

The outgrowth of an enthusiastic passion may take forms such as practice preparation and organization, boundaries and limits that are set in the practice environment, promoting an attitude of civility and respect for each other, the timeliness of the practice plan and the ability to come into the practice environment with a positive attitude.

From my perspective, practice was a time where you could do one of two things—you either get better, or you could get worse. You would never stay the same. This philosophy relates directly to habits and proper practice and how one is motivated to get better on the field of competition. It also relates directly to our spiritual growth, which deserves but very rarely gets daily practice and attention. If we ask ourselves, "Can our players grow physically and get better with one practice a week?" the answer is certainly no! Therefore, how can we expect ourselves to grow spiritually and put our faith into practice with one church service a week and no Bible study, personal reflection, prayer, or the fundamentals of biblical doctrine to complement our growth? The answer is: We cannot.

My suggestion would be to approach your spiritual growth with the same vigor you do your coaching growth. Our passion is determined by our actions. A steady diet of daily prayer, a daily verse card, Bible study, and personal reflection will provide the soul with the spiritual nourishment it needs. The spiritual question is answered in similarity to the physical question—if we practice it correctly, it becomes a way of life.

≫ 6 ≪

BRIDGING THE GAP

*Two are better than one, because they have a good
return for their labor: If either of them falls down,
one can help the other up. But pity anyone who falls
and has no one to help them up. Also, if two lie down
together, they will keep warm. But how can one keep
warm alone? Though one may be overpowered, two
can defend themselves. A cord of three strands is not
quickly broken.*

— Ecclesiastes 4:9–12

Generational Differences

I am a baby boomer, and therefore I see the world from a certain
framework. To further clarify: I was brought up in a two-parent
home with one sibling (an older brother), and my father was a
minister—which got me labeled as a "preacher's kid." The claim
to fame I have on that label is that long ago Dusty Springfield
had a hit song with the chorus, "The only boy who could ever
reach me, was the son of a preacher man." Hopefully my lovely
bride subscribes to that theory.

Not long ago, a colleague of mine and I conducted a
workshop for faculty and staff entitled "Y Me: Teaching and
Coaching the Millennial Generation." To my surprise, we had

a full house of attendees. The basic premise of the hour-and-a-half-long presentation was understanding the mental lens a Y Generation person sees through, as compared to baby boomers like myself or Generation X individuals. We are in a multigenerational workforce, and I believe we are obligated in leadership roles to work on bridging this age gap with effective dialogue from all parties. Each generation has something to offer, and can positively affect communication as we move forward.

So how are we different? Through my experience as a "boomer" in both the coaching field and athletic administration, our views on values, work traits and attributes differ. Through observation, professional work experience, relational experience, and studying I have formed an opinion on what I have seen.

We also must understand that the first of the approximately 78 million boomer retirees out there reached retirement age around 2008. That would leave many still in our workforce following, developing, and implementing policies and/or practice plans that hopefully are benefitting the millennial and beyond.

From a value point of view, the millennial believes in self-expression over self-control. In other words, it is more fun to visibly express perceived accomplishments to others than to maintain an emotional stability. In the athletic world, this can be seen all too often in the highly emotional parts of football and basketball, by the pointing to the sky after a three-pointer or the pounding of the chest after the sacking of the quarterback.

Another value that is not in alignment with each generation is that the "now generation" will respect you only if you earn it. In my formative years, I was always taught to respect the authority of the position automatically. The line of thinking from the millennial is, "First, show me that you are worthy of my respect; you must have credibility; you must show me that you feel I have value."

To address this credibility issue, when meeting with a potential student and their family, I would always arrange the seating in my office a certain way, to highlight not only what had been achieved by past teams but what was important to me. As an example, I would make sure that the family saw a wedding picture of my wife, along with our children, to highlight the importance of family in the student's life. In addition, I would have a shelf of books, not only of successful leaders in sports but positive leaders in other areas of life (i.e., education and business). We know that very few people make money professionally playing sports, so it is important to expose the student to other areas of life. Also, along with my athletic achievements, I would include on a separate wall the most important professional achievement I have received: my doctorate degree, showing that from my perception, advanced education was critical in advancing as a better overall human being.

In relation to the value of people in my recruiting efforts, I would go over what we would provide for them individually from the academic, social, and physical arenas. This assured them I would place a value on their time spent with the program.

Whatever we think of the generation that we coach, these things we do know: They are more globally aware than any generation we have known; they are more technologically advanced; they have several different forms of communication available to them, which they use; and they are adept at marketing themselves. The value of these gifts each athlete possesses, and how they can be used for the overall good, must be an important part of the dialogue, and reinforced throughout the year as we progress in the journey. It must be emphasized that everyone has certain traits that can be recognized for the good of the group.

One example of this, handed down from my mentor, is the award program for certain accomplishments in game-day situations. Each of our players had a nameplate that was attached to his locker as our preseason began. This nameplate was large, with a blank space to utilize a program called the "star award system." During games, we would chart such defensive accomplishments as deflections, going to the floor for 50-50 balls, taking charges, defensive rebounds, and blocked shots. On the offensive end, we would statistically be aware of field-goal and free-throw percentage, offensive rebounds, and assists, along with other offensive categories. Each game would be updated after every game with the appropriate star category, if accomplished. Therefore, the value of the player to the group could be consistently viewed by the team. We even had these categories at some of our team scrimmage practices, so that the players who did not get as much playing time would be able to see their value to the group. Admittedly, this took time and effort. But from our perspective, with the limited staff we had, it was worth it. Ownership means total immersion, or the "both feet in" concept. This method kept us all on task.

Millennials and the boomers differ in attributes as well. Whereas the "now generation" craves change, is more globally aware, and can multitask, the boomer generation was singularly motivated on achieving one goal at a time.

Millennials also differ in their work styles from my generation. Generally, we see a population now that seeks active involvement, wants to be constantly engaged, and is searching for gratification preferably sooner than later. That differs from the singular task-confident, collaborative people I knew from my athletic experience.

No matter how we view the generation we coach or how we categorize them, our principles and core must remain constant and unwavering. We must inspire those we coach to advance in every part of their lives, for them to feel of value. Whether the people we work with agree with our stance as Christian coaches or not, we should not hide from the fact of who we are.

≫ 7 ≪

THE GAME PLAN

How beautiful upon the mountains are the feet of those who bring good news, who proclaim peace; who bring good tidings, who proclaim salvation, who say to Zion, Your God reigns.

— Isaiah 52:7

As coaches, we are very familiar with the game plan. We spend hours viewing tape, going over personnel, and discussing with our staff how to effectively plan a strategy to be successful. And so it is the same with the people we are leading. They look to us for guidance, motivation, encouragement, corrective discipline, education, and discussion. This is where we need to develop our own methods and strategies to impact and influence our athletes for the good. Below are several strategies I tried to incorporate in the development of a competitive healthy culture, not only with my basketball players but also with the staff and colleagues I associated with on a daily basis.

Let Them Know

Evaluation is a part of anything in life, whether it be self-evaluation or, as a coach, evaluating your players. It is extremely important to be open and candid with everyone, focusing on goal-setting, improvement planning, and, just as importantly, what they are doing well. In addition, I believe transparency is key in developing a relationship with the now generation. With social media providing news at the tip of your fingers, it is hard to filter information from seeping into the locker room or clubhouse, whether it is good or bad. This is where you can use your platform power—by meeting with your players at the beginning of the year to go over expectations in relation to their behavior on the field of practice, in the classroom, out in the community, with social media networks, and with the student population. With expectations, there need to be consequences for certain undesirable acts that could adversely affect the individual, coach, team, and school in general.

In addition, it is extremely important to let students know who you are, what motivates and drives you, along with the core values you try to live by—including your faith-based belief. There is nothing wrong with letting them know who you are. Going back to our group core values from Chapter 2, this method of letting them know assists the coach in developing the theme of placing value on his/her players.

Early and definitive communication, which includes expectations and what you will do for them as individuals, is of critical importance. Always stress, and carry through, the commitment to better them as students. Expose them to improvement skills as players both from the physical and cognitive areas, and continue to address and resolve issues that may be a deterrent to their growth as successful human beings. In this way, the player feels more of an intimacy with the coach—and in most cases, will respond in a positive way.

Open-Door Policy

> And to the angel of the church in Philadelphia write;
> These things saith he that is holy, he that is true, he

that hath the key of David, he that openeth, and no
man shutteth; and shutteth, and no man openeth;
I know thy works: behold, I have set before thee an
open door, and no man can shut it: for thou hast a
little strength, and hast kept my word, and hast not
denied my name. (Revelation 3:7–8, KJV)

The above is such a great verse to apply to the Lord's open-
door policy, for us to enter the body of Christ. It does not matter
at what period of our life we decide to make the decision nor
what mistakes we have made; he is willing to allow us to make
the choice to have *faith alone in Christ alone* at any time.

And so it should be with us, as coaches to our players. I
know that many of you at the lower levels of coaching, as I was,
will argue "I'm only part-time and can do only so much." My
response is that if you are willing to own your program, rather
than continually focus on the problem of not being hired for a
full-time effort, you will become a problem-solver. You do this
on the field of competition to give your team the best possible
chance to succeed, so why not provide avenues off the court or
field for students to have one-on-one dialogue with you?

Many times, our success on the court or field is based upon
our continued nurturing of the relationships we have with our
players, not the Xs and Os of the game. By researching ways
to have an open-door policy, you enhance your capabilities of
developing a trustworthy environment. Many times, this would
be after the high emotions of a practice. If you took the time to
speak with two or three players individually after practice, twice
a week, it would help create an environment of consistency, to
better equip players and coaches to trust in each other.

One of the programs I initiated as a head coach was "Lunch
with the Coach." Twice a month during the academic year, I
would have lunch with a member of the team. The rule was

that we could not talk about basketball in the hour or so we had together. Discussions could cover school work, family, emotional or social issues, and/or spirituality. This avenue provided a mechanism for both the player and coach to nurture the different areas of their relationship, and hopefully a development of trust with both. I believe in making oneself available to players and employees, which is important in developing a healthy environment for success.

In the early 1980s a theory defined as "management by walking around" was a buzz phrase on every leader's desk. This method can still be useful today as we lead and manage our own groups of athletes. The premise behind this theory is one of less intimidation and more relational interaction, which will result in the healthy cultural atmosphere we are looking to create. As part of our monthly routine, we visit with each player on our own, discuss ideas to better enhance the overall environment, focus on the positive, and field specific questions that could help develop the trust factor we are looking for in the group culture.

Ask for Feedback

Aside from the open-door policy, where you are involved in one-on-one discussion, feedback is a group trait. Feedback in the practice arena is of critical importance to progressing for the good. Questions, explanations, discussions are all part of keeping players and coaches on the same page. One of our group core values is to encourage the free flow of dialogue. Out of this free flow could come some very quality ideas that you may want to implement. Not long ago, I was observing a basketball practice session. After practice, it was common for this team to come together in a circle with the coaching staff. The circle was enclosed by the group putting their arms around the shoulders of their teammates. This was a time for individuals to speak about practice: what went well, what they needed to improve upon, and the myriad of things that come up in practice. In the end, the coach would summarize what he had heard and they would depart for the evening. I thought, "What a great way to end each practice on an 'all-in' note."

Give Attention to All

Critical to any team success is the fact that we try to get all to buy in to the goals we are trying to establish. Part of this buy-in needs to be created by the coach, and it is important to give attention to every player. Everyone has a certain role and special gift(s) they can utilize to assist in the achievement of team success.

Some people may find this method annoying, particularly self-starters who do not need the coach consistently checking in on them—particularly when things are going well. It is important for the coach to identify those individuals early—and, if they need less attention than the others, recognize and respect that, because all of us have differing views on what it takes to motivate. Sometimes that motivation and inspiration comes from organized meetings, sometimes by a simple word or two, while some are inspired by former players who have gone through similar situations the group is experiencing. Sharing those kinds of personal experiences can help both individuals and groups to develop closer bonds together. Everything we can do to show the group we care about them as human beings goes a long way in creating that camaraderie needed in a healthy, effective, and successful unit.

This goes back to our core group value of valuing people. It has always been my philosophy that we may make mistakes in our recruiting process; however, while we are with the people that we have recruited, it is our obligation to try and get the best of what they should offer.

Empower the Athlete

There are many ways to empower the athlete. In my most recent position, we chose as a staff to complement our community-service activities (which most programs do), adding two in-house activities for our students to participate in. I have found that by empowering the individual, he begins to take responsibility, which is so important to success and accountability.

In the first case, our staff decided to provide workshops to a select group of athletes, empowering them to develop a project together with their peers (other athletes) for the betterment of the program. As a group, they decided on the project, what timeline would need to be followed, and when the group would finish. They would come to the coaching staff for direction, but the results were on them. It was such a thrill to watch them work together as a team, and function with their special skill set beyond the field of competition.

The second initiative involved the education process of becoming young adults and taking responsibility for their own actions. Workshops and PowerPoint presentations, along with other visual presentations, were given on a variety of subjects including compliance, respect, civility, sports and the global influence, the body functioning as one, accountability, the social network, and commitment.

My hope in these endeavors was that we would create a culture of sustainability, showing our students how much we valued them. These kinds of endeavors also created dialogue on both sides and the free flow of ideas.

When NFL coach and general manager Bill Parcells was inducted into the Hall of Fame, he was asked the question of what responsibility he felt in leading the young multimillionaire men under his tutelage—not only by being successful on the field, but how to achieve off the field. His response was that he felt it was his obligatory responsibility to try, but he was not responsible for the final product. This goes to the direct point of empowering individuals with the tools to achieve; however, the final accountability is up to them. Our players and people under our supervision are responsible for the choices they make, resulting in direct accountability.

Focus on the Process

To get to the result, we must continue to focus on the process. What will it take to get us to the vision we have defined? This is a tedious task that takes time and plenty of effort on everyone's part. Often it takes time to change the model of thinking, so that there is an alignment as to what the group is trying to accomplish. The uniqueness about the two-year-college level is that players are trying to develop their individual skills so that they can move on to the four-year college or university. In many cases, it is not only the developing of physical skills but also academic and life skills (socially and emotionally). That must be part of our process in helping our young people. Continuing to focus on the process will assist in the later outcome, whether it be winning on the field of competition or winning as successful human beings and citizens.

Incorporate Social Time

With all the pressure and stress that go along with the athletic journey, it is critical to have what I call the "no pressure zone." Create a safe environment where your athletes can have down time together, and focus more on their hobbies or things they enjoy together.

Establish Team Traditions

This is highly important in the bonding phase of a team, or department for that matter. One of the traditions handed down from my mentor was simply called "the hill." During our preseason, we would begin the training process with our conditioning program, which included running outdoors, along with weight training in the fitness center. The players didn't enjoy the outdoor conditioning so much because it was a combination of distance and interval running, sprints, and the dreaded hill. This exercise was done for two weeks, where we would utilize different venues, rain or shine. All our running was done out of doors before the official start of practice on October 1. We would do traditional running such as interval, sprints, and distance, but two or three times during that period we would go to the local community sledding hill and have our session at this venue.

"The Hill" was located on a local river that ran through the community, and it had a steady incline to get to the top. The goal would be to make it to the top in a certain time—several times in a row. Once that was accomplished, we would do some other running and return to "The Hill" for another set. After the preseason running period was over, those who had completed "The Hill" were awarded T-shirts that said, "I Survived the Hill," with a graphic of an athlete struggling up to the top. These T-shirts were like badges of courage, and included stories to go along with them. It became a great bonding effort, as many times we would see those more gifted in their mental toughness assisting others through encouragement, motivation, and even at times dragging them along.

Create an Atmosphere of Respect

Each year, for the past eight years, I have provided workshops to our athletes on an area that seems to be lost in our dealings with other human beings: civility and respect. This presentation includes sections to empower the individual to create his own world of respecting others, including definitions of words that are used throughout the presentation such as social, respect, trust, civility, humility, and passion. We defined these words for the athletes, so that when they were used in the presentation we were all functioning under those definitions. With this set of common terms in place, we then concentrated on specific areas such as the social network and how it can be a positive or disruptive influence in our lives; social behavior on and off campus; rules to follow on the subject of civility and respect; factors that tarnish the ability to exhibit civility and respect; how to seize opportunities to show respect for others; and finally, what we like to call the Midas Touch— the ability to take the focus off of yourself and celebrate the accomplishment of others.

I would like to point out that five of the major religions in the world have something about respect and civility in their doctrinal principles:

> Do unto others as you would have them do unto you (Christianity).
>
> No one of you is a believer until he loves for his neighbor what he loves for himself (Islam).
>
> Hurt not others with that which pains yourself (Buddhism).
>
> What is hateful to you, do not do to your fellow man. This is the entire Law; all the rest is commentary (Judaism).
>
> Do not unto others what you would not have them do unto you (Hinduism.)

I find it interesting that each doctrine has something in it that addresses the issue of treating others with respect and civility. And yet it is so difficult for many of us to get to that point in our lives (including myself, at times).

To create a healthy competitive culture, try incorporating the above action items with your team. Concentrating on the above areas will assist you in becoming highly focused in your skills to lead, and will show your players that you value each one of them, as a spoke that gives the wheel momentum.

≫ 8 ≪

BEING BROUGHT TO AWARENESS

*According as his divine power hath given unto us all
things that [pertain] unto life and godliness, through
the knowledge of him that hath called us to glory
and virtue.*

— 2 Peter 1:3 (KJV)

The longer I have coached and worked as an athletic director, the more evident it has become to me that my mental lens
needed to be stretched and expanded, to include the capacity
of the diverse ways of thinking and processing that people go
through to lead their own lives. This revelation has allowed me
to not necessarily accept different lines of thought in relation to
how I lead myself; nonetheless, it has opened me to understand
that what motivates one person is not necessarily what motivates another.

I have seen three specific benefits from this. First, this
stretching of the mental lens allowed evaluation of myself
daily—truly thinking about my actions during the day and how
I treated other fellow human beings—which was something
I had not done before. This evaluation process was a direct
influence on my becoming more disciplined within my own
life. I have become more focused, and more of an individual

who utilizes and maximizes my daily schedule. This is not to say that I do not still do some mindless things, but I am now more cognizant of continuous quality improvement.

Secondly, and as mentioned in Chapter 1, this journey has assisted me in clarifying core values that are important to my daily living patterns. Values such as solid moral character, honesty, integrity, authenticity, transparency, passion, and humility jump to the forefront when I think about my daily improvement—and believe me, it is a daily challenge on my part to adhere to these types of values; many times, I fall short.

It is my humble opinion that truly effective leadership has, and always will, start with the way that someone leads themselves. I believe the ethical challenge we all face is not only *knowing* what is right and wrong, but having the moral courage to *do* the right thing. This ethical challenge, and the courage to act appropriately, is an obligation that must be passed on to the people we are fortunate enough to have in our care. I also believe that if someone is Christ-centered, these core values may come easier. They are continuously spoken about in Scripture, and the closer one draws to Scripture and the inculcation that takes place by metabolizing the correct interpretation of the Scripture, the more the divine view begins to permeate through an individual.

Thirdly, I would say this athletic journey of mine has brought me to a point of humility—understanding that, in many cases, I am learning as much from our athletes as they are from me.

A Personal Relationship

In the process of my doctoral journey, a team of survey monitors and I conducted a study of 145 two-year college student athletes to determine, among other things, what they were looking for in a relationship with their coach. In the qualitative portion of the study, many significant findings were realized through interviews and written questionnaires. As I share some of these quotes from students, I will categorize them into what I believe are statements concerning certain expectations the "Y Generation" is searching for in their relationship with their coach. Although we cannot generalize that this is what every student-athlete is looking for, we can say these are general themes in today's athletic culture that should be noticed—and possibly accommodated to—in the hopes of motivating the player. Let's take a look briefly at some of the quotes we obtained, categorized for convenience:

Intimacy/Closeness

"I think a coach that is personable is an effective coach."

"Every coach needs to find out more about the player's activity off the field."

"The coach should have more team-bonding activities to show she cares."

"Coaches should be personal with the players off the field. He should have some level of understanding of what is going on in the lives of each individual player."

"Being able to connect with the players and have a good time is very important. However, they [the coach] need to be able to control the players as well when it is time to work."

Flexibility/Awareness/Decision-making

"Provide necessary changes in the lineup."

"If team is not improving in games or in practice the coach should change something to possibly help them win."

"A coach has certain guidelines that should be followed, but the coach needs to ascertain ways for different players to get the best out of them. Some need to be encouraged, other players need to be pushed, and so on. A good coach can deal with adversity and must be able to change."

Fairness/Justice

"The coach should have confidence in everyone and not just certain players. Don't have favorites."

"Coaches should try to avoid favoring certain players on the team more than others."

Effective Communication

"I think communication should be talked about because communication is the key in any sport. Also, coaches should give as much respect as they get from their players."

"If your coach is a man and you are playing women's sports, I strongly feel that your coach should understand that women are more emotional than men."

Respect

"I think it is important for coaches to earn the respect of the players, not just expect it, not just think they deserve it because of their position."

Accountability/Shared Responsibility

"Although athletes are the producers, coaches play as big a role as the athlete just in a different aspect."

"Every coach is different and I think you need to have a love for the game itself and being on a team and working with others. Not all coaches I've had have had those qualities but being able to teach myself has made me a stronger player."

Positive Reinforcement

"Coaches need to be excited and tell the players good comments when the team or players do good things."

As can be seen from these quotes, there are differing opinions from our student athletes. However, some general themes that can be deduced. Certainly, there is a desire to have a personal relationship with the coach. This would tend to indicate that, in some cases, the athlete is not receiving the personal touch from a nurturing home environment, and that the desire is to be (and feel) close to someone in all aspects of their lives.

Secondly, we find that there needs to be some flexibility in coaching methods, and a better awareness of what is going on— not only with each individual, but in relationship to the overall team dynamic.

In addition, we find a general theme of fairness and a just attitude. A coach who is perceived in this way seems to be in a better position to not only motivate and inspire athletes, but also better influence them in appropriate and ethical conduct.

To address this issue of personal relationship, the school I recently retired from as athletic director initiated a program called the Student Athlete Leadership Team (S.A.L.T.—our motto is "S.A.L.T. Is Good for You"). With this group of fifteen students, chosen by their coaches, we have begun the journey of trying to develop leaders through formal training methods. Although S.A.L.T. has taken part in many community-service activities during the last three years, this training is much more than the "good works" philosophy. These students meet once a month in a formalized workshop and have been provided teachings on Intrapersonal Leadership, Servant Leadership, Commitment, Teamwork, Unity, Embracing Adversity, and The Domino Effect of Decision-Making. The above Student Athlete Leadership Team was a result of an awareness I had come to, from the aforementioned study and some general themes that came out of that research.

Relationships are always about being aware of what the members of the group need, in order to motivate and inspire them. I have found through the years that the more I listened to and communicated with my players, staff, and colleagues, the more I became aware of what they valued and needed, not only in their individual professional lives but also as a group. Words and phrases like intimacy, flexibility, fairness, effective communication, accountability, shared responsibility, and respect are actions that we should reflect upon daily, to keep ourselves aware of what is good for the group.

❯ 9 ❮

THE WILL SKILL

*Cast your cares on the LORD and he will sustain you; he
will never let the righteous be shaken.*

— Psalm 55:22

She was a girly girl from a young age. Always dressed so feminine and fresh, she cared about her cleanliness, took care of her nails, toes, face, and hair meticulously. She was proud of who she was, and she has always made me feel like a ridiculous overachiever not only in her looks but her unconditional loving grace and attitude.

But one thing she was not: She was never an athlete. She did the right things in the exercise and nutritional areas, but she never had the natural grace, balance, strength, or incredible coordination that are often associated with athletic excellence. Although she was at peace with who she was, she also wanted to be called an athlete at some point in time.

Not long ago she decided to get a personal trainer. As she began her training, I could tell she was becoming more excited about going. At one point in her training she said, "I'm going to sign up for the Spartan Race." Initiated around 2013, The Spartan Race developed by Reebok is an international event. This specific event took place on December 5, 2015, and was a five-mile course with thirty-five different obstacles to clear before the finish—wall climbing, carrying cement balls over waist-high water without allowing the ball to be buoyed by the water, jumping over burning flames, crawling under barbed wire fencing and a multitude of others.

The day of the event came, and as we drove to the race early in the morning a weather system had settled in south Florida where we lived—the kind of system that just circles around in place for hours on end. This certainly complicated the situation, as when we arrived, the entire course was either underwater or extremely muddy. The rain would never let up that day, but the race would go on. There were more than four thousand people who participated. They were set off into large groups to negotiate—or should I say, battle—the five-mile course.

My words as a spectator will never appropriately explain what she went through, as I could only imagine the fight she had on her hands trying to complete the course in what was basically a torrential downpour. Five miles—and some two hours and twenty minutes later—she came toward me in this downpour. I had thrown my umbrella away hours ago because it did no good. As she walked toward me drenched with mud, muck, bug bites, cuts, and bruises, you could tell she was exhausted but "juiced." You know that feeling—the one you get when you hit a game-winning shot, or a walkoff hit, or a final kill in a five-set thriller in volleyball. The feeling you get when you just have completed something you never thought you could do. I recognized the passion just oozing out of her veins as she talked; words were coming out of her mouth a mile a minute. But the one thing she said—so simple a statement, yet so profound in meaning to her—was "I did it!" She had her doubts before the event, and certainly during it, but her will would not allow her to quit. If she was moving, she was finishing—just like her "will skill" had kept her moving when she raised two children on her own to become college graduates, all while holding down a full-time job and getting her master's degree.

To say the least, she slept well that night. The next morning as we awoke and she rehashed the event to me, I noticed something else that provided the analogy I am about to point out: Her body was filled with bruises, cuts, and bug bites, and her knee was severely swollen with fluid. There were so many bruises that I thought she had invented a more economical way of tattooing. But she wore them like a badge of courage. When she found one she hadn't noticed, she would make sure, with a slight smile and a twinkle in her eye, to show me.

As you may have guessed by now, my story is about my wife! And by the way, the day after the event she went and got her hair done, along with her nails, toes, and a much-deserved massage. She was, again, a girly girl.

I came to the realization that my wife's battered body signified life as we know it. We all start at ground zero and begin working our way up, to achieving that goal, whatever it may be. We are in the Rocky Mountains most of the time. We climb these peaks that are goals, and along the way we get knocked down, battered, bruised, emotionally cut so deep that we want to quit. The people who survive and succeed dust themselves off, because their will does not allow them to quit. Their determination and "will skill" always figures out a way to find solutions, and thus more of a resolve to carry on. Whether it is in our athletic, academic, social, or spiritual life, the will skill must be a conscious choice, because it is not a natural talent; it is a choice we make to keep pushing forward. We embrace adversity, because we understand that without difficult times there is no growth. We cannot grow as mature human beings without trial. If we choose to have the will skill, our rewards will far exceed our expectations. A person who has elite physical talent but little will skill will never maximize their capacity to achieve, whereas an individual who possesses some physical talent but incredible will skill will achieve far beyond their expectations. The elite in any capacity of life have tremendous talent, coupled with an indestructible will.

Another one of my favorite stories concerns a former player of mine. In the middle of my coaching career, we had a basketball team that was mainly a core of freshman. We had a very successful regular season, posting a 25–6 record and being ranked in the top fifteen in the country. However, in postseason play, we were upset in the regional semifinals, never realizing the dream of playing against the best in the country at the national tournament.

After that season, one of my freshmen decided to stop attending school. No matter what we did as a staff, he just would not get the job done. With about a month left in the semester I brought him in and told him we would not be re-signing him for the following year, due to his lack of effort in the classroom. He debated me, but the decision was final and he was out.

In June of that year, he called me up; he told me he was currently enrolled in summer school in his hometown and would be coming back to play basketball at the college. I told him he could do whatever he wanted, and that it was admirable he was going to summer school, but we were not in need of him and he should look for another school to attend in the fall semester.

Brushing aside my discouragement, he showed up in my office for the fall semester and said he would try out for the team. He had worked and gone to school in the summer, getting enough money to pay for his schooling and getting himself academically eligible. I told him he was welcome to try out for the team—as we were taking two non-scholarship players—but that we had so much talent that even if he made the team, he would not play. Basically, I told him, he was wasting a year of athletic eligibility.

I could not discourage his "will skill." In the end, he became a starter as our third guard on a team that again ranked in the top fifteen in the country—and this time made it to the Final Four in the country, being defeated by the eventual national champions by two points in the semifinal game. To finish his story, he attended a small four-year university in the Midwest, finished his basketball playing career, and received his bachelor's degree.

People who will not surrender when they have obstacles laid in front of them, or have created them on their own, inevitably find a way to accomplish something that remains meaningful in their lives.

And so, it is with our Christian conviction. We should not shy away, and we should not surrender. Our core makes us who we are, and we have an obligation to take the journey in good grace, determination, and passion.

≫ |0 ≪

THE WITNESS

My mouth shall tell of Your righteousness, of your
salvation all day long, though I know not its measure.

— Psalm 71:15

In the end, leading oneself in a positive influencing way is the most difficult challenge we face as coaches. When we view what goes on around us—the unethical behavior, the misrepresenting of the truth, the "looking the other way" at inappropriate behavior—there is a tendency, if we are not true leaders, to follow suit and say "everybody does it." This type of attitude perpetuates a vicious cycle of leading not only yourself, but others, into the shady and dark areas of the sports community where the philosophy is "anything goes," as long as we win. What can you do to positively impact your small part of the sport community?

Let us now reflect on ourselves and identify the core that we should be seeking in this volatile world of athletics. If we are men and women of a Christian faith, we must start with a faith-based belief that Jesus Christ was the son of God; and that when he went to the cross, he imputed all the sins of mankind past, present, and future. It is by his grace and his grace alone that we are saved—and that is a flat-out gift! We are nothing without him. The only requirement is that we must believe.

Once we have done this, we have a core within us that must be developed—just as you would develop a perimeter player in the teachings of how to effectively pass the ball to the post or interior. That maturation of our faith, through the fundamentals, will enable us to evolve from the inside. This maturation will make us able to not only lean on Scripture through adversity and challenges, but recall the appropriate Scripture at the right time.

Centering on faith-based principles also allows us to defend our soul against false teachings and "protect our basket," so to speak. Our mere fundamental practice of knowing and believing the Scripture will allow us the freedom of going through days with a relaxed mental attitude. Our growth out of faith-based principles, as we mature, will eventually transfer characteristics such as passion, humility, empathy, compassion, patience, endurance, flexibility, examinational reflection, competitiveness, poise, ethical behavior, and positive volitional choice. This will allow us as coaches to have the capacity and ability to set boundaries and constructively correct players, without them losing their respect or self-esteem.

To simplify, let's look at this from our world of athletics. As coaches, we are consistently driving into our players the fundamentals of the game, not only from the physical sense but from an intelligence viewpoint. We want them to get to the point that during the game they are free to play because they have been so well-schooled. Our players do not need to necessarily think before they do something; they are proactive, and just respond to the situation in the correct manner. How do we get them to that point? It is my belief that through correct and constant repetition in the day-to-day fundamentals, we free our players. We use a variety of drills and ways to reinforce the same things, but that is what we are trying to do—we are truly trying to free our players to go play.

This philosophy reminds me of a segment of an essay written by Pulitzer prize-winner David Maraniss entitled "The Coach Who Wasn't There." In one part of the essay, Maraniss is writing about legendary NFL coach Vince Lombardi, of whom he says:

> The phrase most often attributed to Lombardi is winning isn't everything, it is the only thing. Lombardi was a contradictory man inside a simple exterior; an imperfect figure driving for perfection in others. I disagreed with him on many things, but on one philosophical idea I found I learned more from him than I ever expected. It is the idea of freedom through discipline. That is, the only way to be free is to discipline yourself to master the world around you. With Lombardi, his players were disciplined to learn the Packer sweep, one running play over and over, every practice every day, but they practiced it so often and learned all the possible variations of it and defensive responses to it so thoroughly that it became not a matter of rote but of intuition. They could see everything more clearly, as if in slow motion, so that once a game started, they had tremendous freedom to react. That philosophy of freedom through discipline kept them one step ahead of their opponents. What is true for football players also holds true for other professions, even ones that on the surface might seem different. A jazz musician becomes free through the discipline of knowing the music, it is only then that his improvisations become great. And so it is with a writer. Just as his old players were different people when they finished playing for him, I felt I was a different person when I finished writing about him.

This philosophy should be practiced by us, as men and women of a Christian faith who have been put in front of a group of athletes. We must first listen to the biblical information that is given to us, digest it just as we would food nutrients for the physical body (metabolize), and allow it to become our way of life (inculcate). Once these faith-based principles have become part of our everyday life, it will free us to live out our core and positively meet the everyday challenges of coaching.

Interestingly, as we evaluate ourselves and critically analyze who we are as Christian coaches, does it not make sense that to get better in our spiritual lives we must address our own souls daily, so that we can better utilize the incredible tools that have been given to us by God? The great thing about what we have available is found in one book, the Bible! We do not have to go to search engines, which can lead down thousands of different avenues, to find what we are looking for. Our solution is found in one book.

Outgrowths of witnessing can be utilized in your everyday association with your players, by integrating some of who you are with your interactions during practice, in the classroom, and in one-on-one engagement. As an example, I have had the opportunity to be able to be an athletic director, teacher, and head coach all at the same time. I can remember beginning each class or session with a passage from the Bible, and offering students the interpretation of that verse and how it was relevant to their daily lives. I would always point out that even if they had no belief in God or Jesus Christ as his son, that by going to this one source (the Bible) they could find the tools to live a great life! In addition, our locker room was always the site of a prayer before the game—not to necessarily win the game but to play up to our capability, and to ask for grace and mercy to keep all from serious injury and harm.

The most difficult part of witnessing with our passion is to always supplement and complement your Christian dialogue with your actions. Does this mean that you don't show your emotion, anger, frustration, or disappointment? Absolutely not! Those characteristics are part of human nature, and from my humble view it is a sign of the caring a coach has for his or her team that these emotions come out. Our stumbling block as coaches is that often we forget what a joy it is to see a team become a unit that grows and bonds together. We often do not show joy, excitement, and enthusiasm in the mere process and journey that we are taking with our students.

In the end, it becomes about the journey, because our spiritual life aligns many times with our athletic journey, our Rocky Mountains—trying consistently to reach spiritual maturity as we try to reach the summit in our athletic journey.

It is important to remember this as we go through the Christian spiritual journey. We cannot let one of the most evident sins that crops up as we grow and mature in the word of God: arrogance! We must remember that the closer we get to divine thinking, the more we feel we have all the right answers. Let us understand that we, in the body of Christ, are the witness. We will all be judged at a time that is suitable to God. Our mission is to not judge, but to witness! That does not mean that we do not evaluate and make choices on how we should live our lives, but it is not the intent of Jesus to send us out as judges. We are to be his witnesses.

The great apostle Paul said it best: "I have fought the good fight, I have finished the race, I have kept the faith" (2 Tim. 4:7). And ultimately—from our Christian faith, and as Christian coaches—this verse sums our journey up, because we all want to hear in that great eternal life that is ours to come, "Well done, good and faithful servant!" (Matt. 25:21).

About the Author

David Holstein is the recently retired Director of Athletics at Palm Beach State College in Lake Worth, Florida. He has been immersed in two-year college athletics as an athlete, assistant coach, head coach, and athletic director for nearly four decades.

Dr. Holstein earned his EdD in Ethical Leadership from Olivet Nazarene University, completing his dissertation, "College Athletes' Perceptions of Effective Coaching Behaviors and How Perceptions Influence Individual Performance and Team Satisfaction," in May of 2010.

He has been involved in student services work at the two-year college level his entire professional career, serving as a student activities coordinator, career planning and placement counselor, academic advisor, assistant men's basketball coach, head men's basketball coach, and athletic director. His perspectives are based on these experiences as well as athletic studies that he has read.

During his thirteen years as a head coach, his teams were involved in eight National Junior College Athletic Association (NJCAA) Region 4 championships, winning four titles. His 2000 team went to the Final Four of the NJCAA national men's basketball tournament. He has mentored seven NJCAA All-Americans and placed over 70 of his players at NCAA Division I or Division II Universities.

In March of 2008, Dr. Holstein was voted into the National Junior College Athletic Association Region 4 Hall of Fame as an AD/Coach. He has been the Sports Chair of the Florida College System Activities Association Council for Athletic Affairs of the

Southern Conference and a member of the Florida Council for Athletic Affairs Executive Board for two-year colleges.

Dr. David B. Holstein and his wife, Cynthia, have their roots in the Midwest as they both grew up in Kankakee, Illinois, but now reside in Florida. They have five grown children: Wesley, David, Heidi, Carlye, and Madelyn.